Emily Dickinson

Selected by
Helen McNeil

PHOENIX
POETRY

This edition first published in Everyman in 1996
Phoenix edition first published 2002

Selection © J. M. Dent 1996
Chronology © J. M. Dent 2002

ISBN: 0 7538 1 659 8

Typeset by Deltatype Ltd
Birkenhead, Merseyside

Printed in China by
South China Printing Co. Ltd.

A CIP catalogue reference for this book
is available from the British Library.

The Orion Publishing Group
Orion House
5 Upper St Martin's Lane
London
WC2H 9EA

Contents

Poems

Emily Dickinson

67

Success is counted sweetest
By those who ne'er succeed.
To comprehend a nectar
Requires sorest need.

Not one of all the purple Host
Who took the Flag today
Can tell the definition
So clear of Victory

As he defeated – dying –
On whose forbidden ear
The distant strains of triumph
Burst agonized and clear!

187

How many times these low feet staggered –
Only the soldered mouth can tell –
Try – can you stir the awful rivet –
Try – can you lift the hasps of steel!

Stroke the cool forehead – hot so often –
Lift – if you care – the listless hair –
Handle the adamantine fingers
Never a thimble – more – shall wear –

Buzz the dull flies – on the chamber window –
Brave – shines the sun through the freckled pane –
Fearless – the cobweb swings from the ceiling –
Indolent Housewife – in Daisies – lain!

193

I shall know why – when Time is over –
And I have ceased to wonder why –
Christ will explain each separate anguish
In the fair schoolroom of the sky –

He will tell me what "Peter" promised –
And I – for wonder at his woe –
I shall forget the drop of Anguish
That scalds me now – that scalds me now!

199

I'm "wife" – I've finished that –
That other state –
I'm Czar – I'm "Woman" now –
It's safer so –

How odd the Girl's life looks
Behind this soft Eclipse –
I think that Earth feels so
To folks in Heaven – now –

This being comfort – then
That other kind – was pain –
But why compare?
I'm "Wife"! Stop there!

211

Come slowly — Eden!
Lips unused to Thee —
Bashful — sip thy Jessamines —
As the fainting Bee —

Reaching late his flower,
Round her chamber hums —
Counts his nectars —
Enters — and is lost in Balms.

214

I taste a liquor never brewed —
From Tankards scooped in Pearl —
Not all the Vats upon the Rhine
Yield such an Alcohol!

Inebriate of Air — am I —
And Debauchee of Dew —
Reeling — thro endless summer days —
From inns of Molten Blue —

When 'Landlords' turn the drunken Bee
Out of the Foxglove's door —
When Butterflies — renounce their ''drams'' —
I shall but drink the more!

Till Seraphs swing their snowy Hats
And Saints — to windows run —
To see the little Tippler
Leaning against the — Sun —

216

Safe in their Alabaster Chambers –
Untouched by Morning
And untouched by Noon –
Sleep the meek members of the Resurrection –
Rafter of satin,
And Roof of stone.

Light laughs the breeze
In her Castle above them –
Babbles the Bee in a stolid Ear,
Pipe the Sweet Birds in ignorant cadence –
Ah, what sagacity perished here!

VERSION OF 1859

Safe in their Alabaster Chambers –
Untouched by Morning –
And untouched by Noon –
Lie the meek members of the Resurrection –
Rafter of Satin – and Roof of Stone!

Grand go the Years – in the Crescent – above them –
Worlds scoop their Arcs –
And Firmaments – row –
Diadems – drop – and Doges – surrender –
Soundless as dots – on a Disc of Snow –

VERSION OF 1861

225

Jesus! thy Crucifix
Enable thee to guess
The smaller size!

Jesus! thy second face
Mind thee in Paradise
Of ours!

228

Blazing in Gold and quenching in Purple
Leaping like Leopards to the Sky
Then at the feet of the old Horizon
Laying her spotted Face to die
Stooping as low as the Otter's Window
Touching the Roof and tinting the Barn
Kissing her Bonnet to the Meadow
And the Juggler of Day is gone

239

"Heaven" – is what I cannot reach!
The Apple on the Tree –
Provided it do hopeless – hang –
That – "Heaven" is – to Me!

The Color, on the Cruising Cloud –
The interdicted Land –
Behind the Hill – the House behind –
There – Paradise – is found!

Her teasing Purples – Afternoons –
The credulous – decoy –
Enamored – of the Conjuror –
That spurned us – Yesterday!

241

I like a look of Agony,
Because I know it's true –
Men do not sham Convulsion,
Nor simulate, a Throe –

The Eyes glaze once – and that is Death –
Impossible to feign
The Beads upon the Forehead
By homely Anguish strung.

243

I've known a Heaven, like a Tent –
To wrap its shining Yards –
Pluck up its stakes, and disappear –
Without the sound of Boards
Or Rip of Nail – Or Carpenter –
But just the miles of Stare –
That signalize a Show's Retreat –
In North America –

No Trace – no Figment of the Thing
That dazzled, Yesterday,
No Ring – no Marvel –
Men, and Feats –
Dissolved as utterly –
As Bird's far Navigation
Discloses just a Hue –
A plash of Oars, a Gaiety –
Then swallowed up, of View.

248

Why — do they shut Me out of Heaven?
Did I sing — too loud?
But — I can say a little "Minor"
Timid as a Bird!

Wouldn't the Angels try me —
Just — once — more —
Just — see — if I troubled them —
But don't — shut the door!

Oh, if I — were the Gentleman
In the "White Robe" —
And they — were the little Hand — that knocked —
Could — I — forbid?

249

Wild Nights — Wild Nights!
Were I with thee
Wild Nights should be
Our luxury!

Futile — the Winds —
To a Heart in port —
Done with the Compass —
Done with the Chart!

Rowing in Eden —
Ah, the Sea!
Might I but moor — Tonight —
In Thee!

250

I shall keep singing!
Birds will pass me
On their way to Yellower Climes –
Each – with a Robin's expectation –
I – with my Redbreast –
And my Rhymes –

Late – when I take my place in summer –
But – I shall bring a fuller tune –
Vespers – are sweeter than Matins – Signor –
Morning – only the seed of Noon –

251

Over the fence –
Strawberries – grow –
Over the fence –
I could climb – if I tried, I know –
Berries are nice!

But – if I stained my Apron –
God would certainly scold!
Oh, dear, – I guess if He were a Boy –
He'd – climb – if He could!

252

I can wade Grief –
Whole Pools of it –
I'm used to that –
But the least push of Joy
Breaks up my feet –
And I tip – drunken –
Let no Pebble – smile –
'Twas the New Liquor –
That was all!

Power is only Pain –
Stranded, thro' Discipline,
Till Weights – will hang –
Give Balm – to Giants –
And they'll wilt, like Men –
Give Himmaleh –
They'll Carry – Him!

254

"Hope" is the thing with feathers –
That perches in the soul –
And sings the tune without the words –
And never stops – at all –

And sweetest – in the Gale – is heard –
And sore must be the storm –
That could abash the little Bird
That kept so many warm –

I've heard it in the chillest land –
And on the strangest Sea –
Yet, never, in Extremity,
It asked a crumb – of Me.

258

There's a certain Slant of light,
Winter Afternoons –
That oppresses, like the Heft
Of Cathedral Tunes –

Heavenly Hurt, it gives us –
We can find no scar,
But internal difference,
Where the Meanings, are –

None may teach it – Any –
'Tis the Seal Despair –
An imperial affliction
Sent us of the Air –

When it comes, the Landscape listens –
Shadows – hold their breath –
When it goes, 'tis like the Distance
On the look of Death –

271

A solemn thing – it was – I said –
A woman – white – to be –
And wear – if God should count me fit –
Her blameless mystery –

A hallowed thing – to drop a life
Into the purple well –
Too plummetless – that it return –
Eternity – until –

I pondered how the bliss would look –
And would it feel as big –
When I could take it in my hand –
As hovering – seen – through fog –

And then – the size of this "small" life –
The Sages – call it small –
Swelled – like Horizons – in my vest –
And I sneered – softly – "small"!

273

He put the Belt around my life –
I heard the Buckle snap –
And turned away, imperial,
My Lifetime folding up –
Deliberate, as a Duke would do
A Kingdom's Title Deed –
Henceforth, a Dedicated sort –
A Member of the Cloud.

Yet not too far to come at call –
And do the little Toils
That make the Circuit of the Rest –
And deal occasional smiles
To lives that stoop to notice mine –
And kindly ask it in –
Whose invitation, know you not
For Whom I must decline?

274

The only Ghost I ever saw
Was dressed in Mechlin – so –
He wore no sandal on his foot –
And stepped like flakes of snow –

His Gait – was soundless, like the Bird –
But rapid – like the Roe –
His fashions, quaint, Mosaic –
Or haply, Mistletoe –

His conversation – seldom –
His laughter, like the Breeze –
That dies away in Dimples
Among the pensive Trees –

Our interview – was transient –
Of me, himself was shy –
And God forbid I look behind –
Since that appalling Day!

280

I felt a Funeral, in my Brain,
And Mourners to and fro
Kept treading – treading – till it seemed
That Sense was breaking through –

And when they all were seated,
A Service, like a Drum –
Kept beating – beating – till I thought
My Mind was going numb –

And then I heard them lift a Box
And creak across my Soul
With those same Boots of Lead, again,
Then Space — began to toll,

As all the Heavens were a Bell,
And Being, but an Ear,
And I, and Silence, some strange Race
Wrecked, solitary, here —

And then a Plank in Reason, broke,
And I dropped down, and down —
And hit a World, at every plunge,
And Finished knowing — then —

285

The Robin's my Criterion for Tune —
Because I grow — where Robins do —
But, were I Cuckoo born —
I'd swear by him —
The ode familiar — rules the Noon —
The Buttercup's, my Whim for Bloom —
Because, we're Orchard sprung —
But, were I Britain born,
I'd Daisies spurn —
None but the Nut — October fit —
Because, through dropping it,
The Seasons flit — I'm taught —
Without the Snow's Tableau
Winter, were lie — to me —
Because I see — New Englandly —
The Queen, discerns like me —
Provincially —

288

I'm Nobody! Who are you?
Are you – Nobody – Too?
Then there's a pair of us?
Don't tell! they'd advertise – you know!

How dreary – to be – Somebody!
How public – like a Frog –
To tell one's name – the livelong June –
To an admiring Bog!

291

How the old Mountains drip with Sunset
How the Hemlocks burn –
How the Dun Brake is draped in Cinder
By the Wizard Sun –

How the old Steeples hand the Scarlet
Till the Ball is full –
Have I the lip of the Flamingo
That I dare to tell?

Then, how the Fire ebbs like Billows –
Touching all the Grass
With a departing – Sapphire – feature –
As a Duchess passed –

How a small Dusk crawls on the Village
Till the Houses blot
And the odd Flambeau, no men carry
Glimmer on the Street –

How it is Night – in Nest and Kennel –
And where was the Wood –
Just a Dome of Abyss is Bowing
Into Solitude –

These are the Visions flitted Guido –
Titian – never told –
Domenichino dropped his pencil –
Paralyzed, with Gold –

303

The Soul selects her own Society –
Then – shuts the Door –
To her divine Majority –
Present no more –

Unmoved – she notes the Chariots – pausing –
At her low Gate –
Unmoved – an Emperor be kneeling
Upon her Mat –

I've known her – from an ample nation –
Choose One –
Then – close the Valves of her attention –
Like Stone –

311

It sifts from Leaden Sieves –
It powders all the Wood.
It fills with Alabaster Wool
The Wrinkles of the Road –

It makes an Even Face
Of Mountain, and of Plain –
Unbroken Forehead from the East
Unto the East again –

It reaches to the Fence –
It wraps it Rail by Rail
Till it is lost in Fleeces –
It flings a Crystal Vail

On Stump – and Stack – and Stem –
A Summer's empty Room –
Acres of Joints – where Harvests were,
Recordless but for them –

It Ruffles Wrists of Posts
As Ankles of a Queen –
Then stills its Artisans – like Ghosts –
Denying they have been –

312

Her – "last Poems" –
Poets – ended –
Silver – perished – with her Tongue –
Not on Record – bubbled other,
Flute – or Woman –
So divine –
Not unto its Summer – Morning
Robin – uttered Half the Tune –
Gushed too free for the Adoring –
From the Anglo-Florentine –
Late – the Praise –
'Tis dull – conferring

On the Head too High to Crown –
Diadem – or Ducal Showing –
Be its Grave – sufficient sign –
Nought – that We – No Poet's Kinsman –
Suffocate – with easy woe –
What, and if, Ourself a Bridegroom –
Put Her down – in Italy?

315

He fumbles at your Soul
As Players at the Keys
Before they drop full Music on –
He stuns you by degrees –
Prepares your brittle Nature
For the Ethereal Blow
By fainter Hammers – further heard –
Then nearer – Then so slow
Your Breath has time to straighten –
Your Brain – to bubble Cool –
Deals – One – imperial – Thunderbolt –
That scalps your naked Soul –

When Winds take Forests in their Paws –
The Universe – is still –

320

We play at Paste –
Till qualified, for Pearl –
Then, drop the Paste –
And deem ourself a fool –

The Shapes — though — were similar —
And our new Hands
Learned *Gem*-Tactics —
Practicing *Sands* —

322

There came a Day at Summer's full,
Entirely for me —
I thought that such were for the Saints,
Where Resurrections — be —

The Sun, as common, went abroad,
The flowers, accustomed, blew,
As if no soul the solstice passed
That maketh all things new —

The time was scarce profaned, by speech —
The symbol of a word
Was needless, as at Sacrament,
The Wardrobe — of our Lord —

Each was to each The Sealed Church,
Permitted to commune this — time —
Lest we too awkward show
At Supper of the Lamb.

The Hours slid fast — as Hours will,
Clutched tight, by greedy hands —
So faces on two Decks, look back,
Bound to opposing lands —

And so when all the time had leaked,
Without external sound
Each bound the Other's Crucifix —
We gave no other Bond —

Sufficient troth, that we shall rise –
Deposed – at length, the Grave –
To that new Marriage,
Justified – through Calvaries of Love –

324

Some keep the Sabbath going to Church –
I keep it, staying at Home –
With a Bobolink for a Chorister –
And an Orchard, for a Dome –

Some keep the Sabbath in Surplice –
I just wear my Wings –
And instead of tolling the Bell, for Church,
Our little Sexton – sings.

God preaches, a noted Clergyman –
And the sermon is never long,
So instead of getting to Heaven, at last –
I'm going, all along.

326

I cannot dance upon my Toes –
No Man instructed me –
But oftentimes, among my mind,
A Glee possesseth me,

That had I Ballet knowledge –
Would put itself abroad
In Pirouette to blanch a Troupe –
Or lay a Prima, mad,

And though I had no Gown of Gauze –
No Ringlet, to my Hair,
Nor hopped to Audiences – like Birds,
One Claw upon the Air,

Nor tossed my shape in Eider Balls,
Nor rolled on wheels of snow
Till I was out of sight, in sound,
The House encore me so –

Nor any know I know the Art
I mention – easy – Here –
Nor any Placard boast me –
It's full as Opera –

327

Before I got my eye put out
I liked as well to see –
As other Creatures, that have Eyes
And know no other way –

But were it told to me – Today –
That I might have the sky
For mine – I tell you that my Heart
Would split, for size of me –

The Meadows – mine –
The Mountains – mine –
All Forests – Stintless Stars –
As much of Noon as I could take
Between my finite eyes –

The Motions of the Dipping Birds –
The Morning's Amber Road –
For mine – to look at when I liked –
The News would strike me dead –

So safer – guess – with just my soul
Upon the Window pane –
Where other Creatures put their eyes –
Incautious – of the Sun –

338

I know that He exists.
Somewhere – in Silence –
He has hid his rare life
From our gross eyes.

'Tis an instant's play.
'Tis a fond Ambush –
Just to make Bliss
Earn her own surprise!

But – should the play
Prove piercing earnest –
Should the glee – glaze –
In Death's – stiff – stare –

Would not the fun
Look too expensive!
Would not the jest –
Have crawled too far!

341

After great pain, a formal feeling comes –
The Nerves sit ceremonious, like Tombs –
The stiff Heart questions was it He, that bore,
And Yesterday, or Centuries before?

The Feet, mechanical, go round –
Of Ground, or Air, or Ought –
A Wooden way
Regardless grown,
A Quartz contentment, like a stone –

This is the Hour of Lead –
Remembered, if outlived,
As Freezing persons, recollect the Snow –
First – Chill – then Stupor – then the letting go –

365

Dare you see a Soul *at the White Heat?*
Then crouch within the door –
Red – is the Fire's common tint –
But when the vivid Ore
Has vanquished Flame's conditions,
It quivers from the Forge
Without a color, but the light
Of unanointed Blaze.
Least Village has its Blacksmith
Whose Anvil's even ring
Stands symbol for the finer Forge
That soundless tugs – within –
Refining these impatient Ores
With Hammer, and with Blaze

Until the Designated Light
Repudiate the Forge –

374

I went to Heaven –
'Twas a small Town –
Lit – with a Ruby –
Lathed – with Down –

Stiller – than the fields
At the full Dew –
Beautiful – as Pictures –
No Man drew.
People – like the Moth –
Of Mechlin – frames –
Duties – of Gossamer –
And Eider – names –
Almost – contented –
I – could be –
'Mong such unique
Society –

378

I saw no Way – The Heavens were stitched –
I felt the Columns close –
The Earth reversed her Hemispheres –
I touched the Universe –

And back it slid – and I alone –
A Speck upon a Ball –
Went out upon Circumference –
Beyond the Dip of Bell –

389

There's been a Death, in the Opposite House,
As lately as Today —
I know it, by the numb look
Such Houses have — alway —

The Neighbors rustle in and out —
The Doctor — drives away —
A Window opens like a Pod —
Abrupt — mechanically —

Somebody flings a Mattress out —
The Children hurry by —
They wonder if it died — on that —
I used to — when a Boy —

The Minister — goes stiffly in —
As if the House were His —
And He owned all the Mourners — now —
And little Boys — besides —

And then the Milliner — and the Man
Of the Appalling Trade —
To take the measure of the House —

There'll be that Dark Parade —

Of Tassels — and of Coaches — soon —
It's easy as a Sign —
The Intuition of the News —
In just a Country Town —

391

A Visitor in Marl –
Who influences Flowers –
Till they are orderly as Busts –
And Elegant – as Glass –

Who visits in the Night –
And just before the Sun –
Concludes his glistening interview –
Caresses – and is gone –

But whom his fingers touched –
And where his feet have run –
And whatsoever Mouth he kissed –
Is as it had not been –

401

What Soft – Cherubic Creatures –
These Gentlewomen are –
One would as soon assault a Plush –
Or violate a Star –

Such Dimity Convictions –
A Horror so refined
Of freckled Human Nature –
Of Deity – ashamed –

It's such a common – Glory –
A Fisherman's – Degree –
Redemption – Brittle Lady –
Be so – ashamed of Thee –

414

'Twas like a Maelstrom, with a notch,
That nearer, every Day,
Kept narrowing its boiling Wheel
Until the Agony

Toyed coolly with the final inch
Of your delirious Hem –
And you dropt, lost,
When something broke –
And let you from a Dream –

As if a Goblin with a Gauge –
Kept measuring the Hours –
Until you felt your Second
Weigh, helpless, in his Paws –

And not a Sinew – stirred – could help,
And sense was setting numb –
When God – remembered – and the Fiend
Let go, then, Overcome –

As if your Sentence stood – pronounced –
And you were frozen led
From Dungeon's luxury of Doubt
To Gibbets, and the Dead –

And when the Film had stitched your eyes
A Creature gasped "Reprieve"!
Which Anguish was the utterest – then –
To perish, or to live?

425

Good Morning – Midnight –
I'm coming Home –
Day – got tired of Me –
How could I – of Him?

Sunshine was a sweet place –
I liked to stay –
But Morn – didn't want me – now –
So – Goodnight – Day!

I can look – can't I –
When the East is Red?
The Hills – have a way – then –
That puts the Heart – abroad –

You – are not so fair – Midnight –
I chose – Day –
But – please take a little Girl –
He turned away!

435

Much Madness is divinest Sense –
To a discerning Eye –
Much Sense – the starkest Madness –
'Tis the Majority
In this, as All, prevail –
Assent – and you are sane –
Demur – you're straightway dangerous –
And handled with a Chain –

441

This is my letter to the World
That never wrote to Me —
The simple News that Nature told —
With tender Majesty

Her Message is committed
To Hands I cannot see —
For love of Her — Sweet — countrymen —
Judge tenderly — of Me

448

This was a Poet — It is That
Distills amazing sense
From ordinary Meanings —
And Attar so immense

From the familiar species
That perished by the Door —
We wonder it was not Ourselves
Arrested it — before —

Of Pictures, the Discloser —
The Poet — it is He —
Entitles Us — by Contrast —
To ceaseless Poverty —

Of Portion — so unconscious —
The Robbing — could not harm —
Himself — to Him — a Fortune —
Exterior — to Time —

449

I died for Beauty – but was scarce
Adjusted in the Tomb
When One who died for Truth, was lain
In an adjoining Room –

He questioned softly "Why I failed"?
"For Beauty", I replied –
"And I – for Truth – Themself are One –
We Brethren, are", He said –

And so, as Kinsmen, met a Night –
We talked between the Rooms –
Until the Moss had reached our lips –
And covered up – our names –

451

The Outer – from the Inner
Derives its Magnitude –
'Tis Duke, or Dwarf, according
As is the Central Mood –

The fine – unvarying Axis
That regulates the Wheel –
Though Spokes – spin – more conspicuous
And fling a dust – the while.

The Inner paints the Outer –
The Brush without the Hand –
Its Picture publishes – precise –
As is the inner Brand

On fine – Arterial Canvas –
A Cheek – perchance a Brow –
The Star's whole Secret – in the Lake –
Eyes were not meant to know.

454

It was given to me by the Gods –
When I was a little Girl –
They give us Presents most – you know –
When we are new – and small.
I kept it in my Hand –
I never put it down –
I did not care to eat – or sleep –
For fear it would be gone –
I heard such words as "Rich" –
When hurrying to school –
From lips at Corners of the Streets –
And wrestled with a smile.
Rich! 'Twas Myself – was rich –
To take the name of Gold –
And Gold to own – in solid Bars –
The Difference – made me bold –

462

Why make it doubt – it hurts it so –
So sick – to guess –
So strong – to know –
So brave – upon its little Bed
To tell the very last They said

Unto Itself − and smile − And shake −
For that dear − distant − dangerous − Sake −
But − the Instead − the Pinching fear
That Something − it did do − or dare −
Offend the Vision − and it flee −
And They no more remember me −
Nor ever turn to tell me why −
Oh, Master, This is Misery −

465

I heard a Fly buzz − when I died −
The Stillness in the Room
Was like the Stillness in the Air −
Between the Heaves of Storm −

The Eyes around − had wrung them dry −
And Breaths were gathering firm
For that last Onset − when the King
Be witnessed − in the Room −

I willed my Keepsakes − Signed away
What portion of me be
Assignable − and then it was
There interposed a Fly −

With Blue − uncertain stumbling Buzz −
Between the light − and me −
And then the Windows failed − and then
I could not see to see −

475

Doom is the House without the Door –
'Tis entered from the Sun –
And then the Ladder's thrown away,
Because Escape – is done –

'Tis varied by the Dream
Of what they do outside –
Where Squirrels play – and Berries die –
And Hemlocks – bow – to God –

479

She dealt her pretty words like Blades –
How glittering they shone –
And every One unbared a Nerve
Or wantoned with a Bone –

She never deemed – she hurt –
That – is not Steel's Affair –
A vulgar grimace in the Flesh –
How ill the Creatures bear –

To Ache is human – not polite –
The Film upon the eye
Mortality's old Custom –
Just locking up – to Die.

486

I was the slightest in the House —
I took the smallest Room —
At night, my little Lamp, and Book —
And one Geranium —

So stationed I could catch the Mint
That never ceased to fall —
And just my Basket —
Let me think — I'm sure
That this was all —

I never spoke — unless addressed —
And then, 'twas brief and low —
I could not bear to live — aloud —
The Racket shamed me so —

And if it had not been so far —
And any one I knew
Were going — I had often thought
How noteless — I could die —

489

We pray — to Heaven —
We prate — of Heaven —
Relate — when Neighbors die —
At what o'clock to Heaven — they fled —
Who saw them — Wherefore fly?

Is Heaven a Place — a Sky — a Tree?
Location's narrow way is for Ourselves —
Unto the Dead
There's no Geography —

But State – Endowal – Focus –
Where – Omnipresence – fly?

492

Civilization – spurns – the Leopard!
Was the Leopard – bold?
Deserts – never rebuked her Satin –
Ethiop – her Gold –
Tawny – her Customs –
She was Conscious –
Spotted – her Dun Gown –
This was the Leopard's nature – Signor –
Need – a keeper – frown?

Pity – the Pard – that left her Asia –
Memories – of Palm –
Cannot be stifled – with Narcotic –
Nor suppressed – with Balm –

501

This World is not Conclusion.
A Species stands beyond –
Invisible, as Music –
But positive, as Sound –
It beckons, and it baffles –
Philosophy – don't know –
And through a Riddle, at the last –
Sagacity, must go –
To guess it, puzzles scholars –
To gain it, Men have borne

Contempt of Generations
And Crucifixion, shown –
Faith slips – and laughs, and rallies –
Blushes, if any see –
Plucks at a twig of Evidence –
And asks a Vane, the way –
Much Gesture, from the Pulpit –
Strong Hallelujahs roll –
Narcotics cannot still the Tooth
That nibbles at the soul –

Fascicle 17

348

I dreaded that first Robin, so,
But He is mastered, now,
I'm some accustomed to Him grown,
He hurts a little, though —

I thought if I could only live
Till that first Shout got by —
Not all Pianos in the Woods
Had power to mangle me —

I dared not meet the Daffodils —
For fear their Yellow Gown
Would pierce me with a fashion
So foreign to my own —

I wished the Grass would hurry —
So — when 'twas time to see —
He'd be too tall, the tallest one
Could stretch — to look at me —

I could not bear the Bees should come,
I wished they'd stay away
In those dim countries where they go,
What word had they, for me?

They're here, though; not a creature failed —
No Blossom stayed away
In gentle deference to me —
The Queen of Calvary —

Each one salutes me, as he goes,
And I, my childish Plumes,
Lift, in bereaved acknowledgment
Of their unthinking Drums —

505

I would not paint — a picture —
I'd rather be the One
Its bright impossibility
To dwell — delicious — on —
And wonder how the fingers feel
Whose rare — celestial — stir —
Evokes so sweet a Torment —
Such sumptuous — Despair —

I would not talk, like Cornets —
I'd rather be the One
Raised softly to the Ceilings —
And out, and easy on —
Through Villages of Ether —
Myself endued Balloon
By but a lip of Metal —
The pier to my Pontoon —

Nor would I be a Poet —
It's finer — own the Ear —
Enamored — impotent — content —
The License to revere,
A privilege so awful
What would the Dower be,
Had I the Art to stun myself
With Bolts of Melody!

506

He touched me, so I live to know
That such a day, permitted so,
I groped upon his breast –
It was a boundless place to me
And silenced, as the awful sea
Puts minor streams to rest.

And now, I'm different from before,
As if I breathed superior air –
Or brushed a Royal Gown –
My feet, too, that had wandered so –
My Gypsy face – transfigured now –
To tenderer Renown –

Into this Port, if I might come,
Rebecca, to Jerusalem,
Would not so ravished turn –
Nor Persian, baffled at her shrine
Lift such a Crucifixal sign
To her imperial Sun.

349

I had the Glory – that will do –
An Honor, Thought can turn her to
When lesser Fames invite –
With one long "Nay" –
Bliss' early shape
Deforming – Dwindling – Gulfing up –
Time's possibility.

507

She sights a Bird — she chuckles —
She flattens — then she crawls —
She runs without the look of feet —
Her eyes increase to Balls —

Her Jaws stir — twitching — hungry —
Her Teeth can hardly stand —
She leaps, but Robin leaped the first —
Ah, Pussy, of the Sand,

The Hopes so juicy ripening —
You almost bathed your Tongue —
When Bliss disclosed a hundred Toes —
And fled with every one —

350

They leave us with the Infinite.
But He — is not a man —
His fingers are the size of fists —
His fists, the size of men —

And whom he foundeth, with his Arm
As Himmaleh, shall stand —
Gibraltar's Everlasting Shoe
Poised lightly on his Hand,

So trust him, Comrade —
You for you, and I, for you and me
Eternity is ample,
And quick enough, if true.

508

I'm ceded — I've stopped being Theirs —
The name They dropped upon my face
With water, in the country church
Is finished using, now,
And They can put it with my Dolls,
My childhood, and the string of spools,
I've finished threading — too —

Baptized, before, without the choice,
But this time, consciously, of Grace —
Unto supremest name —
Called to my Full — The Crescent dropped —
Existence's whole Arc, filled up,
With one small Diadem.

My second Rank — too small the first —
Crowned — Crowing — on my Father's breast —
A half unconscious Queen —
But this time — Adequate — Erect,
With Will to choose, or to reject,
And I choose, just a Crown —

509

If anybody's friend be dead
It's sharpest of the theme
The thinking how they walked alive —
At such and such a time —

Their costume, of a Sunday,
Some manner of the Hair –
A prank nobody knew but them
Lost, in the Sepulchre –

How warm, they were, on such a day,
You almost feel the date –
So short way off it seems –
And now – they're Centuries from that –

How pleased they were, at what you said –
You try to touch the smile
And dip your fingers in the frost –
When was it – Can you tell –

You asked the Company to tea –
Acquaintance – just a few –
And chatted close with this Grand Thing
That don't remember you –

Past Bows, and Invitations –
Past Interview, and Vow –
Past what Ourself can estimate –
That – makes the Quick of Woe!

510

It was not Death, for I stood up,
And all the Dead, lie down –
It was not Night, for all the Bells
Put out their Tongues, for Noon.

It was not Frost, for on my Flesh
I felt Siroccos – crawl –
Nor Fire – for just my Marble feet
Could keep a Chancel, cool –

And yet, it tasted, like them all,
The Figures I have seen
Set orderly, for Burial,
Reminded me, of mine –

As if my life were shaven,
And fitted to a frame,
And could not breathe without a key,
And 'twas like Midnight, some –

When everything that ticked – has stopped –
And Space stares all around –
Or Grisly frosts – first Autumn morns,
Repeal the Beating Ground –

But, most, like Chaos – Stopless – cool –
Without a Chance, or Spar –
Or even a Report of Land –
To justify – Despair.

511

If you were coming in the Fall,
I'd brush the Summer by
With half a smile, and half a spurn,
As Housewives do, a Fly.

If I could see you in a year,
I'd wind the months in balls –
And put them each in separate Drawers,
For fear the numbers fuse –

If only Centuries, delayed,
I'd count them on my Hand,
Subtracting, till my fingers dropped
Into Van Dieman's Land.

If certain, when this life was out –
That yours and mine, should be
I'd toss it yonder, like a Rind,
And take Eternity –

But, now, uncertain of the length
Of this, that is between,
It goads me, like the Goblin Bee –
That will not state – its sting.

351

I felt my life with both my hands
To see if it was there –
I held my spirit to the Glass,
To prove it possibler –

I turned my Being round and round
And paused at every pound
To ask the Owner's name –
For doubt, that I should know the Sound –

I judged my features – jarred my hair –
I pushed my dimples by, and waited –
If they – twinkled back –
Conviction might, of me –

I told myself, "Take Courage, Friend –
That – was a former time –
But we might learn to like the Heaven,
As well as our Old Home!"

352

Perhaps I asked too large –
I take – no less than skies –
For Earths, grow thick as
Berries, in my native town –

My Basket holds – just – Firmaments –
Those – dangle easy – on my arm,
But smaller bundles – Cram.

328

A Bird, came down the Walk –
He did not know I saw –
He bit an Angleworm in halves
And ate the fellow, raw,

And then, he drank a Dew
From a convenient Grass –
And then hopped sidewise to the Wall
To let a Beetle pass –

He glanced with rapid eyes
That hurried all around –
They looked like frightened Beads, I thought –
He stirred his Velvet Head

Like one in danger, Cautious,
I offered him a Crumb
And he unrolled his feathers
And rowed him softer home –

Than Oars divide the Ocean,
Too silver for a seam —
Or Butterflies, off Banks of Noon
Leap, plashless as they swim.

512

The Soul has Bandaged moments —
When too appalled to stir —
She feels some ghastly Fright come up
And stop to look at her —

Salute her — with long fingers —
Caress her freezing hair —
Sip, Goblin, from the very lips
The Lover — hovered — o'er —
Unworthy, that a thought so mean
Accost a Theme — so — fair —

The soul has moments of Escape —
When bursting all the doors —
She dances like a Bomb, abroad,
And swings upon the Hours,

As do the Bee — delirious borne —
Long Dungeoned from his Rose —
Touch liberty — then know no more,
But Noon, and Paradise —

The Soul's retaken moments —
When, Felon led along,
With shackles on the plumed feet,
And staples, in the Song,

The Horror welcomes her, again,
These, are not brayed of Tongue –

513

Like Flowers, that heard the news of Dews,
But never deemed the dripping prize
Awaited their – low Brows –

Or Bees – that thought the Summer's name
Some rumour of Delirium,
No Summer – could – for Them –

Or Arctic Creatures, dimly stirred –
By Tropic Hint – some Travelled Bird
Imported to the Word –

Or Wind's bright signal to the Ear –
Making that homely, and severe,
Contented, known, before –

The Heaven – unexpected come,
To Lives that thought the Worshipping
A too presumptuous Psalm –

END OF FASCICLE 17

518

Her sweet Weight on my Heart a Night
Had scarcely deigned to lie –
When, stirring, for Belief's delight,
My Bride had slipped away –

48

If 'twas a Dream — made solid — just
The Heaven to confirm —
Or if Myself were dreamed of Her —
The power to presume —

With Him remain — who unto Me —
Gave — even as to All —
A Fiction superseding Faith —
By so much — as 'twas real —

520

I started Early — Took my Dog —
And visited the Sea —
The Mermaids in the Basement
Came out to look at me —

And Frigates — in the Upper Floor
Extended Hempen Hands —
Presuming Me to be a Mouse —
Aground — upon the Sands —

But no Man moved Me — till the Tide
Went past my simple Shoe —
And past my Apron — and my Belt
And past my Bodice — too —

And made as He would eat me up —
As wholly as a Dew
Upon a Dandelion's Sleeve —
And then — I started — too —

And He — He followed — close behind —
I felt his Silver Heel
Upon my Ankle — Then my Shoes
Would overflow with Pearl —

Until We met the Solid Town –
No One He seemed to know –
And bowing – with a Mighty look –
At me – The Sea withdrew –

528

Mine – by the Right of the White Election!
Mine – by the Royal Seal!
Mine – by the Sign in the Scarlet prison –
Bars – cannot conceal!

Mine – here – in Vision – and in Veto!
Mine – by the Grave's Repeal –
Titled – Confirmed –
Delirious Charter!
Mine – long as Ages steal!

536

The Heart asks Pleasure – first –
And then – Excuse from Pain –
And then – those little Anodynes
That deaden suffering –

And then – to go to sleep –
And then – if it should be
The will of its Inquisitor
The privilege to die –

544

The Martyr Poets – did not tell –
But wrought their Pang in syllable –
That when their mortal name be numb –
Their mortal fate – encourage Some –
The Martyr Painters – never spoke –
Bequeathing – rather – to their Work –
That when their conscious fingers cease –
Some seek in Art – the Art of Peace –

546

To fill a Gap
Insert the Thing that caused it –
Block it up
With Other – and 'twill yawn the more –
You cannot solder an Abyss
With Air.

547

I've seen a Dying Eye
Run round and round a Room –
In search of Something – as it seemed –
Then Cloudier become –
And then – obscure with Fog –
And then – be soldered down
Without disclosing what it be
'Twere blessed to have seen –

569

I reckon – when I count at all –
First – Poets – Then the Sun –
Then Summer – Then the Heaven of God –
And then – the List is done –

But, looking back – the First so seems
To Comprehend the Whole –
The Others look a needless Show –
So I write – Poets – All –

Their Summer – lasts a Solid Year –
They can afford a Sun
The East – would deem extravagant –
And if the Further Heaven –

Be Beautiful as they prepare
For Those who worship Them –
It is too difficult a Grace –
To justify the Dream –

570

I could die – to know –
'Tis a trifling knowledge –
News-Boys salute the Door –
Carts – joggle by –
Morning's bold face – stares in the window –
Were but mine – the Charter of the least Fly –

Houses hunch the House
With their Brick Shoulders —
Coals — from a Rolling Load — rattle — how — near —
To the very Square — His foot is passing —
Possibly, this moment —
While I — dream — Here —

572

Delight — becomes pictorial —
When viewed through Pain —
More fair — because impossible
That any gain —

The Mountain — at a given distance —
In Amber — lies —
Approached — the Amber flits — a little —
And That's — the Skies —

575

"Heaven" has different Signs — to me —
Sometimes, I think that Noon
Is but a symbol of the Place —
And when again, at Dawn,

A mighty look runs round the World
And settles in the Hills —
An Awe if it should be like that
Upon the Ignorance steals —

The Orchard, when the Sun is on –
The Triumph of the Birds
When they together Victory make –
Some Carnivals of Clouds –

The Rapture of a finished Day –
Returning to the West –
All these – remind us of the place
That Men call "Paradise" –

Itself be fairer – we suppose –
But how Ourself, shall be
Adorned, for a Superior Grace –
Not yet, our eyes can see –

581

I found the words to every thought
I ever had – but One –
And that – defies me –
As a Hand did try to chalk the Sun

To Races – nurtured in the Dark –
How would your own – begin?
Can Blaze be shown in Cochineal –
Or Noon – in Mazarin?

585

I like to see it lap the Miles –
And lick the Valleys up –
And stop to feed itself at Tanks –
And then – prodigious step

Around a Pile of Mountains —
And supercilious peer
In Shanties — by the sides of Roads —
And then a Quarry pare

To fit its Ribs
And crawl between
Complaining all the while
In horrid — hooting stanza —
Then chase itself down Hill —

And neigh like Boanerges —
Then — punctual as a Star
Stop — docile and omnipotent
At its own stable door —

587

Empty my Heart, of Thee —
Its single Artery —
Begin, and leave Thee out —
Simply Extinction's Date —

Much Billow hath the Sea —
On Baltic — They —
Subtract Thyself, in play,
And not enough of me
Is left — to put away —
"Myself" meant Thee —

Erase the Root — no Tree —
Thee — then — no me —
The Heavens stripped —
Eternity's vast pocket, picked —

593

I think I was enchanted
When first a sombre Girl —
I read that Foreign Lady —
The Dark — felt beautiful —

And whether it was noon at night —
Or only Heaven — at Noon —
For very Lunacy of Light
I had not power to tell —

The Bees — became as Butterflies —
The Butterflies — as Swans
Approached — and spurned the narrow Grass —
And just the meanest Tunes

That Nature murmured to herself
To keep herself in Cheer —
I took for Giants — practising
Titanic Opera —

The Days — to Mighty Metres stept —
The Homeliest — adorned
As if unto a Jubilee
'Twere suddenly confirmed —

I could not have defined the change —
Conversion of the Mind
Like Sanctifying in the Soul —
Is witnessed — not explained —

'Twas a Divine Insanity
The Danger to be Sane
Should I again experience —
'Tis Antidote to turn —

To Tomes of solid Witchcraft —
Magicians be asleep —
But Magic — hath an Element
Like Deity — to keep —

599

There is a pain — so utter —
It swallows substance up —
Then covers the Abyss with Trance —
So Memory can step
Around — across — upon it —
As one within a Swoon —
Goes safely — where an open eye —
Would drop Him — Bone by Bone.

601

A still — Volcano — Life —
That flickered in the night —
When it was dark enough to do
Without erasing sight —

A quiet — Earthquake Style —
Too subtle to suspect
By natures this side Naples —
The North cannot detect

The Solemn — Torrid — Symbol —
The lips that never lie —
Whose hissing Corals part — and shut —
And Cities — ooze away —

606

The Trees like Tassels — hit — and swung —
There seemed to rise a Tune
From Miniature Creatures
Accompanying the Sun —

Far Psalteries of Summer —
Enamoring the Ear
They never yet did satisfy —
Remotest — when most fair

The Sun shone whole at intervals —
Then Half — then utter hid —
As if Himself were optional
And had Estates of Cloud

Sufficient to enfold Him
Eternally from view —
Except it were a whim of His
To let the Orchards grow —

A Bird sat careless on the fence —
One gossipped in the Lane
On silver matters charmed a Snake
Just winding round a Stone —

Bright Flowers slit a Calyx
And soared upon a Stem
Like Hindered Flags — Sweet hoisted —
With Spices — in the Hem —

'Twas more — I cannot mention —
How mean — to those that see —
Vandyke's Delineation
Of Nature's — Summer Day!

607

Of nearness to her sundered Things
The Soul has special times —
When Dimness — looks the Oddity —
Distinctness — easy — seems —

The Shapes we buried, dwell about,
Familiar, in the Rooms —
Untarnished by the Sepulchre,
The Mouldering Playmate comes —

In just the Jacket that he wore —
Long buttoned in the Mold
Since we — old mornings, Children — played —
Divided — by a world —

The Grave yields back her Robberies —
The Years, our pilfered Things —
Bright Knots of Apparitions
Salute us, with their wings —

As we — it were — that perished —
Themself — had just remained till we rejoin them —
And 'twas they, and not ourself
That mourned.

613

They shut me up in Prose —
As when a little Girl
They put me in the Closet —
Because they liked me "still" —

Still! Could themself have peeped —
And seen my Brain — go round —
They might as wise have lodged a Bird
For Treason — in the Pound —

Himself has but to will
And easy as a Star
Abolish his Captivity —
And laugh — No more have I —

617

Don't put up my Thread and Needle —
I'll begin to Sew
When the Birds begin to whistle —
Better Stitches — so —

These were bent — my sight got crooked —
When my mind — is plain
I'll do seams — a Queen's endeavor
Would not blush to own —

Hems — too fine for Lady's tracing
To the sightless Knot —
Tucks — of dainty interspersion —
Like a dotted Dot —

Leave my Needle in the furrow —
Where I put it down —
I can make the zigzag stitches
Straight — when I am strong —

Till then — dreaming I am sewing
Fetch the seam I missed —
Closer — so I — at my sleeping —
Still surmise I stitch —

627

The Tint I cannot take — is best —
The Color too remote
That I could show it in Bazaar —
A Guinea at a sight —

The fine — impalpable Array —
That swaggers on the eye
Like Cleopatra's Company —
Repeated — in the sky —

The Moments of Dominion
That happen on the Soul
And leave it with a Discontent
Too exquisite — to tell —

The eager look — on Landscapes —
As if they just repressed
Some Secret — that was pushing
Like Chariots — in the Vest —

The Pleading of the Summer —
That other Prank — of Snow —
That Cushions Mystery with Tulle,
For fear the Squirrels — know.

Their Graspless manners — mock us —
Until the Cheated Eye
Shuts arrogantly — in the Grave —
Another way — to see —

640

I cannot live with You –
It would be Life –
And Life is over there –
Behind the Shelf

The Sexton keeps the Key to –
Putting up
Our Life – His Porcelain –
Like a Cup –

Discarded of the Housewife –
Quaint – or Broke –
A newer Sevres pleases –
Old Ones crack –

I could not die – with You –
For One must wait
To shut the Other's Gaze down
You – could not –

And I – Could I stand by
And see You – freeze –
Without my Right of Frost –
Death's privilege?

Nor could I rise – with You –
Because Your Face
Would put out Jesus' –
That New Grace

Glow plain – and foreign
On my homesick Eye –
Except that You than He
Shone closer by –

They'd judge Us – How –
For You – served Heaven – You know,
Or sought to –
I could not –

Because You saturated Sight –
And I had no more Eyes,
For sordid excellence
As Paradise

And were You lost, I would be –
Though My Name
Rang loudest
On the Heavenly fame –

And were You – saved –
And I – condemned to be
Where You were not –
That self – were Hell to Me –

So We must meet apart –
You there – I – here –
With just the Door ajar
That Oceans are – and Prayer –
And that White Sustenance –
Despair –

642

Me from Myself – to banish –
Had I Art –
Impregnable my Fortress
Unto All Heart –

But since Myself − assault Me −
How have I peace
Except by subjugating
Consciousness?

And since We're mutual Monarch
How this be
Except by Abdication −
Me − of Me?

646

I think to Live − may be a Bliss
To those who dare to try −
Beyond my limit to conceive −
My lip − to testify −

I think the Heart I former wore
Could widen − till to me
The Other, like the little Bank
Appear − unto the Sea −

I think the Days − could every one
In Ordination stand −
And Majesty − be easier −
Than an inferior kind −

No numb alarm − lest Difference come −
No Goblin − on the Bloom −
No start in Apprehension's Ear,
No Bankruptcy − no Doom −

But Certainties of Sun −
Midsummer − in the Mind −
A steadfast South − upon the Soul −
Her Polar time − behind −

The Vision – pondered long –
So plausible becomes
That I esteem the fiction – real –
The Real – fictitious seems –

How bountiful the Dream –
What Plenty – it would be –
Had all my Life but been Mistake
Just rectified – in Thee

650

Pain – has an Element of Blank –
It cannot recollect
When it begun – or if there were
A time when it was not –

It has no Future – but itself –
Its Infinite contain
Its Past – enlightened to perceive
New Periods – of Pain.

657

I dwell in Possibility –
A fairer House than Prose –
More numerous of Windows –
Superior – for Doors –

Of Chambers as the Cedars –
Impregnable of Eye –
And for an Everlasting Roof
The Gambrels of the Sky –

Of Visitors – the fairest –
For Occupation – This –
The spreading wide my narrow Hands
To gather Paradise –

670

One need not be a Chamber – to be Haunted –
One need not be a House –
The Brain has Corridors – surpassing
Material Place –

Far safer, of a Midnight Meeting
External Ghost
Than its interior Confronting –
That Cooler Host.

Far safer, through an Abbey gallop,
The Stones a'chase –
Than Unarmed, one's a'self encounter –
In lonesome Place –

Ourself behind ourself, concealed –
Should startle most –
Assassin hid in our Apartment
Be Horror's least.

The Body – borrows a Revolver –
He bolts the Door –
O'erlooking a superior spectre –
Or More –

675

Essential Oils — are wrung —
The Attar from the Rose
Be not expressed by Suns — alone —
It is the gift of Screws —

The General Rose — decay —
But this — in Lady's Drawer
Make Summer — When the Lady lie
In Ceaseless Rosemary —

690

Victory comes late —
And is held low to freezing lips —
Too rapt with frost
To take it —
How sweet it would have tasted —
Just a Drop —
Was God so economical?
His Table's spread too high for Us —
Unless We dine on tiptoe —
Crumbs fit such little mouths —
Cherries — suit Robins —
The Eagle's Golden Breakfast strangles — Them —
God keep His Oath to Sparrows —
Who of little Love — know how to starve —

709

Publication – is the Auction
Of the Mind of Man –
Poverty – be justifying
For so foul a thing

Possibly – but We – would rather
From Our Garret go
White – Unto the White Creator –
Than invest – Our Snow –

Thought belong to Him who gave it –
Then – to Him Who bear
Its Corporeal illustration – Sell
The Royal Air –

In the Parcel – Be the Merchant
Of the Heavenly Grace –
But reduce no Human Spirit
To Disgrace of Price –

711

Strong Draughts of Their Refreshing Minds
To drink – enables Mine
Through Desert or the Wilderness
As bore it Sealed Wine –

To go elastic – Or as One
The Camel's trait – attained –
How powerful the Stimulus
Of an Hermetic Mind –

712

Because I could not stop for Death —
He kindly stopped for me —
The Carriage held but just Ourselves —
And Immortality.

We slowly drove — He knew no haste
And I had put away
My labor and my leisure too,
For His Civility —

We passed the School, where Children strove
At Recess — in the Ring —
We passed the Fields of Gazing Grain —
We passed the Setting Sun —

Or rather — He passed Us —
The Dews drew quivering and chill —
For only Gossamer, my Gown —
My Tippet — only Tulle —

We paused before a House that seemed
A Swelling of the Ground —
The Roof was scarcely visible —
The Cornice — in the Ground —

Since then — 'tis Centuries — and yet
Feels shorter than the Day
I first surmised the Horses' Heads
Were toward Eternity —

721

Behind Me – dips Eternity –
Before Me – Immortality –
Myself – the Term between –

Death but the Drift of Eastern Gray,
Dissolving into Dawn away,
Before the West begin –

'Tis Kingdoms – afterward – they say –
In perfect – pauseless Monarchy –
Whose Prince – is Son of None –
Himself – His Dateless Dynasty –
Himself – Himself diversify –
In Duplicate divine –

'Tis Miracle before Me – then –
'Tis Miracle behind – between –
A Crescent in the Sea –
With Midnight to the North of Her –
And Midnight to the South of Her –
And Maelstrom – in the Sky –

728

Let Us play Yesterday –
I – the Girl at school –
You – and Eternity – the
Untold Tale –

Easing my famine
At my Lexicon –
Logarithm – had I – for Drink –
'Twas a dry Wine –

Somewhat different – must be –
Dreams tint the Sleep –
Cunning Reds of Morning
Make the Blind – leap –

Still at the Egg-life –
Chafing the Shell –
When you troubled the Ellipse –
And the Bird fell –

Manacles be dim – they say –
To the new Free –
Liberty – Commoner –
Never could – to me –

'Twas my last gratitude
When I slept – at night –
'Twas the first Miracle
Let in – with Light –

Can the Lark resume the Shell –
Easier – for the Sky –
Wouldn't Bonds hurt more
Than Yesterday?

Wouldn't Dungeons sorer grate
On the Man – free –
Just long enough to taste –
Then – doomed new –

God of the Manacle
As of the Free –
Take not my Liberty
Away from Me –

741

Drama's Vitallest Expression is the Common Day
That arise and set about Us –
Other Tragedy

Perish in the Recitation –
This – the best enact
When the Audience is scattered
And the Boxes shut –

"Hamlet" to Himself were Hamlet –
Had not Shakespeare wrote –
Though the "Romeo" left no Record
Of his Juliet,

It were infinite enacted
In the Human Heart –
Only Theatre recorded
Owner cannot shut –

754

My Life had stood – a Loaded Gun –
In Corners – till a Day
The Owner passed – identified –
And carried Me away –

And now We roam in Sovereign Woods –
And now We hunt the Doe –
And every time I speak for Him –
The Mountains straight reply –

And do I smile, such cordial light
Upon the Valley glow —
It is as a Vesuvian face
Had let its pleasure through —

And when at Night — Our good Day done —
I guard My Master's Head —
'Tis better than the Eider-Duck's
Deep Pillow — to have shared —

To foe of His — I'm deadly foe —
None stir the second time —
On whom I lay a Yellow Eye —
Or an emphatic Thumb —

Though I than He — may longer live
He longer must — than I —
For I have but the power to kill,
Without — the power to die —

762

The Whole of it came not at once —
'Twas Murder by degrees —
A Thrust — and then for Life a chance —
The Bliss to cauterize —

The Cat reprieves the Mouse
She eases from her teeth
Just long enough for Hope to tease —
Then mashes it to death —

'Tis Life's award — to die —
Contenteder if once —
Than dying half — then rallying
For consciouser Eclipse —

784

Bereaved of all, I went abroad —
No less bereaved was I
Upon a New Peninsula —
The Grave preceded me —

Obtained my Lodgings, ere myself —
And when I sought my Bed —
The Grave it was reposed upon
The Pillow for my Head —

I waked to find it first awake —
I rose — It followed me —
I tried to drop it in the Crowd —
To lose it in the Sea —

In Cups of artificial Drowse
To steep its shape away —
The Grave — was finished — but the Spade
Remained in Memory —

797

By my Window have I for Scenery
Just a Sea — with a Stem —
If the Bird and the Farmer — deem it a "Pine" —
The Opinion will serve — for them —

It has no Port, nor a "Line" — but the Jays —
That split their route to the Sky —
Or a Squirrel, whose giddy Peninsula
May be easier reached — this way —

For Inlands — the Earth is the under side —
And the upper side — is the Sun —
And its Commerce — if Commerce it have —
Of Spice — I infer from the Odors borne —

Of its Voice — to affirm — when the Wind is within —
Can the Dumb — define the Divine?
The Definition of Melody — is —
That Definition is none —

It — suggests to our Faith —
They — suggest to our Sight —
When the latter — is put away
I shall meet with Conviction I somewhere met
That Immortality —

Was the Pine at my Window a ''Fellow
Of the Royal'' Infinity?
Apprehensions — are God's introductions —
To be hallowed — accordingly —

824

The Wind begun to knead the Grass —
As Women do a Dough —
He flung a Hand full at the Plain —
A Hand full at the Sky —
The Leaves unhooked themselves from Trees —
And started all abroad —
The Dust did scoop itself like Hands —
And throw away the Road —
The Wagons quickened on the Street —
The Thunders gossiped low —
The Lightning showed a Yellow Head —
And then a livid Toe —

The Birds put up the Bars to Nests —
The Cattle flung to Barns —
Then came one drop of Giant Rain —
And then, as if the Hands
That held the Dams — had parted hold —
The Waters Wrecked the Sky —
But overlooked my Father's House —
Just Quartering a Tree —

FIRST VERSION c. 1864

The Wind begun to rock the Grass
With threatening Tunes and low —
He threw a Menace at the Earth —
A Menace at the Sky.

The Leaves unhooked themselves from Trees —
And started all abroad
The Dust did scoop itself like Hands
And threw away the Road.

The Wagons quickened on the Streets
The Thunder hurried slow —
The Lightning showed a Yellow Beak
And then a livid Claw.

The Birds put up the Bars to Nests —
The Cattle fled to Barns —
There came one drop of Giant Rain
And then as if the Hands

That held the Dams had parted hold
The Waters Wrecked the Sky,
But overlooked my Father's House —
Just quartering a Tree —

SECOND VERSION c. 1864

76

861

Split the Lark — and you'll find the Music —
Bulb after Bulb, in Silver rolled —
Scantily dealt to the Summer Morning
Saved for your Ear when Lutes be old.

Loose the Flood — you shall find it patent —
Gush after Gush, reserved for you —
Scarlet Experiment! Sceptic Thomas!
Now, do you doubt that your Bird was true?

875

I stepped from Plank to Plank
A slow and cautious way
The Stars about my Head I felt
About my Feet the Sea.

I knew not but the next
Would be my final inch —
This gave me that precarious Gait
Some call Experience.

889

Crisis is a Hair
Toward which the forces creep
Past which forces retrograde
If it come in sleep

To suspend the Breath
Is the most we can
Ignorant is it Life or Death
Nicely balancing.

Let an instant push
Or an Atom press
Or a Circle hesitate
In Circumference

It – may jolt the Hand
That adjusts the Hair
That secures Eternity
From presenting – Here –

909

I make His Crescent fill or lack –
His Nature is at Full
Or Quarter – as I signify –
His Tides – do I control –

He holds superior in the Sky
Or gropes, at my Command
Behind inferior Clouds – or round
A Mist's slow Colonnade –

But since We hold a Mutual Disc –
And front a Mutual Day –
Which is the Despot, neither knows –
Nor Whose – the Tyranny –

985

The Missing All – prevented Me
From missing minor Things.
If nothing larger than a World's
Departure from a Hinge –
Or Sun's extinction, be observed –
'Twas not so large that I
Could lift my Forehead from my work
For Curiosity.

986

A narrow Fellow in the Grass
Occasionally rides –
You may have met Him – did you not
His notice sudden is –

The Grass divides as with a Comb –
A spotted shaft is seen –
And then it closes at your feet
And opens further on –

He likes a Boggy Acre
A Floor too cool for Corn –
Yet when a Boy, and Barefoot –
I more than once at Noon
Have passed, I thought, a Whip lash
Unbraiding in the Sun
When stooping to secure it
It wrinkled, and was gone –

Several of Nature's People
I know, and they know me –
I feel for them a transport
Of cordiality –

But never met this Fellow
Attended, or alone
Without a tighter breathing
And Zero at the Bone –

1021

Far from Love the Heavenly Father
Leads the Chosen Child,
Oftener through Realm of Briar
Than the Meadow mild.

Oftener by the Claw of Dragon
Than the Hand of Friend
Guides the Little One predestined
To the Native Land.

1071

Perception of an object costs
Precise the Object's loss –
Perception in itself a Gain
Replying to its Price –

The Object Absolute – is nought –
Perception sets it fair
And then upbraids a Perfectness
That situates so far –

1072

Title divine – is mine!
The Wife – without the Sign!
Acute Degree – conferred on me –
Empress of Calvary!
Royal – all but the Crown!
Betrothed – without the swoon
God sends us Women –
When you – hold – Garnet to Garnet –
Gold – to Gold –
Born – Bridalled – Shrouded –
In a Day –
Tri Victory
"My Husband" – women say –
Stroking the Melody –
Is *this* – the way?

1129

Tell all the Truth but tell it slant –
Success in Circuit lies
Too bright for our infirm Delight
The Truth's superb surprise

As Lightning to the Children eased
With explanation kind
The Truth must dazzle gradually
Or every man be blind –

1263

There is no Frigate like a Book
To take us Lands away
Nor any Coursers like a Page
Of prancing Poetry —
This Traverse may the poorest take
Without oppress of Toll —
How frugal is the Chariot
That bears the Human soul.

1304

Not with a Club, the Heart is broken
Nor with a Stone —
A Whip so small you could not see it
I've known

To lash the Magic Creature
Till it fell,
Yet that Whip's Name
Too noble then to tell.

Magnanimous as Bird
By Boy descried —
Singing unto the Stone
Of which it died —

Shame need not crouch
In such an Earth as Ours —
Shame — stand erect —
The Universe is yours.

1311

This dirty — little — Heart
Is freely mine.
I won it with a Bun —
A Freckled shrine —

But eligibly fair
To him who sees
The Visage of the Soul
And not the knees.

1412

Shame is the shawl of Pink
In which we wrap the Soul
To keep it from infesting Eyes —
The elemental Veil
Which helpless Nature drops
When pushed upon a scene
Repugnant to her probity —
Shame is the tint divine.

1498

Glass was the Street — in tinsel Peril
Tree and Traveller stood —
Filled was the Air with merry venture
Hearty with Boys the Road —

Shot the lithe Sleds like shod vibrations
Emphasized and gone
It is the Past's supreme italic
Makes this Present mean —

1515

The Things that never can come back, are several —
Childhood — some forms of Hope — the Dead —
Though Joys — like Men — may sometimes make a
  Journey —
And still abide —
We do not mourn for Traveler, or Sailor,
Their Routes are fair —
But think enlarged of all that they will tell us
Returning here —
"Here!" There are typic "Heres" —
Foretold Locations —
The Spirit does not stand —
Himself — at whatsoever Fathom
His Native Land —

1545

The Bible is an antique Volume —
Written by faded Men
At the suggestion of Holy Spectres —
Subjects — Bethlehem —
Eden — the ancient Homestead —
Satan — the Brigadier —
Judas — the Great Defaulter —
David — the Troubadour —
Sin — a distinguished Precipice
Others must resist —
Boys that "believe" are very lonesome —
Other Boys are "lost" —
Had but the Tale a warbling Teller —

All the Boys would come —
Orpheus' Sermon captivated —
It did not condemn —

1551

Those — dying then,
Knew where they went —
They went to God's Right Hand —
That Hand is amputated now
And God cannot be found —

The abdication of Belief
Makes the Behavior small —
Better an ignis fatuus
Than no illume at all —

1562

Her Losses make our Gains ashamed —
She bore Life's empty Pack
As gallantly as if the East
Were swinging at her Back.
Life's empty Pack is heaviest,
As every Porter knows —
In vain to punish Honey —
It only sweeter grows.

1593

There came a Wind like a Bugle —
It quivered through the Grass
And a Green Chill upon the Heat
So ominous did pass
We barred the Windows and the Doors
As from an Emerald Ghost —
The Doom's electric Moccasin
That very instant passed —
On a strange Mob of panting Trees
And Fences fled away
And Rivers where the Houses ran
Those looked that lived — that Day —
The Bell within the steeple wild
The flying tidings told —
How much can come
And much can go,
And yet abide the World!

1598

Who is it seeks my Pillow Nights —
With plain inspecting face —
"Did you" or "Did you not," to ask —
'Tis "Conscience" — Childhood's Nurse —

With Martial Hand she strokes the Hair
Upon my wincing Head —
"All" Rogues "shall have their part in" what —
The Phosphorus of God —

1601

Of God we ask one favor,
That we may be forgiven —
For what, he is presumed to know —
The Crime, from us, is hidden —
Immured the whole of Life
Within a magic Prison
We reprimand the Happiness
That too competes with Heaven.

1651

A Word made Flesh is seldom
And tremblingly partook
Nor then perhaps reported
But have I not mistook
Each one of us has tasted
With ecstasies of stealth
The very food debated
To our specific strength —

A Word that breathes distinctly
Has not the power to die
Cohesive as the Spirit
It may expire if He —
"Made Flesh and dwelt among us"
Could condescension be
Like this consent of Language
This loved Philology.

1670

In Winter in my Room
I came upon a Worm –
Pink, lank and warm –
But as he was a worm
And worms presume
Not quite with him at home –
Secured him by a string
To something neighboring
And went along.

A Trifle afterward
A thing occurred
I'd not believe it if I heard
But state with creeping blood –
A snake with mottles rare
Surveyed my chamber floor
In feature as the worm before
But ringed with power –

The very string with which
I tied him – too
When he was mean and new
That string was there –

I shrank – "How fair you are"!
Propitiation's claw –
"Afraid," he hissed
"Of me"?
"No cordiality" –
He fathomed me –
Then to a Rhythm Slim
Secreted in his Form
As Patterns swim
Projected him.

That time I flew
Both eyes his way
Lest he pursue
Nor ever ceased to run
Till in a distant Town
Towns on from mine
I set me down
This was a dream.

1705

Volcanoes be in Sicily
And South America
I judge from my Geography –
Volcanoes nearer here
A Lava step at any time
Am I inclined to climb –
A Crater I may contemplate
Vesuvius at Home.

1732

My life closed twice before its close –
It yet remains to see
If Immortality unveil
A third event to me

So huge, so hopeless to conceive
As these that twice befell.
Parting is all we know of heaven,
And all we need of hell.

Chronology of Dickinson's Life

Year	Life
1830	Emily Dickinson born 10 December in Amherst, Massachusetts, USA, the second child of lawyer Edward Dickinson and Emily Norcross Dickinson
1840	Edward sells his half of the family home, The Homestead, and the family moves to another house in Amherst. Emily enters Amherst Academy, where students are taught a 'modern' curriculum including astronomy and pre-Darwinian geology
1842	Her father elected State Senator; re-elected 1843
1846	Religious revival in Amherst; Dickinson expresses doubts to her friend Abiah Root
1847	Enters Mount Holyoke Female Seminary
1848	Withdraws from Mount Holyoke
1850	Another religious revival in Amherst; her father, sister Lavinia and her friend, Susan Gilbert, join First Church of Christ
1851	Travels with her sister to Boston
1852	Her father is elected to the US House of Representatives
1855	Edward moves his family back into The Homestead; Dickinson will stay here for the rest of her life
1858	Writing poetry seriously
1861	*Springfield Republican* prints poem 'I taste a liquor never brewed', altered and titled 'The May-Wine'
1862–3	Writes about 300 poems but undergoes a personal crisis. Shares Amherst's grief for loss of men killed in the Civil War

Chronology of her Times

Year	Literary Context	Historical Events
1830	Stendhal, *Le Rouge et le noir*	Revolutionary uprisings in central Europe
1836	Emerson, 'Nature'	Texas declares independence
1840	Dana, *Two Years Before The Mast* Cooper, *The Pathfinder*	Opium War US population reaches 17 million
1841	Emerson, *Essays, First Series*	John Tyler elected President
1842	Longfellow, *Ballads and Other Poems*	Chartists' second petition
1844	Emerson, *Essays, Second Series*	Telegraph line from Washington to Baltimore
1846	Melville, *Typee*	US-Mexico War
1847	Thackeray, *Vanity Fair* Longfellow, *Evangeline*	Mormons settle in Utah American troops occupy Mexico
1848	Lowell, *Poems and Biglow Papers*	California Gold Rush
1849	Death of Poe	Zachary Taylor elected President
1850	Hawthorne, *The Scarlet Letter*	Death of President Taylor US population reaches 23 million Fugitive Slave Law passed
1851	Melville, *Moby Dick*	Coup d'état in Paris
1852	Stowe, *Uncle Tom's Cabin*	
1855	Whitman, *Leaves of Grass* Longfellow, *Song of Hiawatha*	
1858		Great Eastern launched
1860	Death of Schopenhauer Eliot, *Mill on the Floss*	Abraham Lincoln elected President
1861	Dostoevsky, *Notes from the House of the Dead*	Outbreak of American Civil War
1862		Homestead Act

Year	Life
1864	In Boston for seven months for eye treatment. Two more poems printed
1865	About a thousand poems written by the end of this year
1866	*Springfield Republican* prints 'A narrow Fellow in the Grass' in a much-altered form
1876	Helen Hunt Jackson, Amherst-born poet, becomes literary friend and begs her to publish
1878	'Success is counted sweetest' published anonymously at Jackson's urging
1880	Judge Otis Lord calls frequently at The Homestead and discusses marriage but is turned down
1882	Mother Emily dies
1884	First attack of kidney disease
1886	Dies of kidney disease
1890	First selection of poetry published

Year	Literary Context	Historical Events
1863	Tolstoy, *The Cossacks*	Emancipation proclamation Battle of Gettysburg
1864	Death of Hawthorne	General Sherman captures Savannah
1865	Kipling and Yeats born	Civil War ends Lincoln assassinated
1866	Dostoevsky, *Crime and Punishment*	Fourteenth Amendment Transatlantic cable laid Ulysses S. Grant elected President
1874	Frost, Lowell and Stein born	
1876	Tolstoy, *Anna Karenina* Twain, *Tom Sawyer*	Bell's speaking telephone Battle of Little Big Horn
1880	Wallace Stevens born	Boer uprising in Transvaal
1882	Death of Emerson	
1885	Twain, *Huckleberry Finn*	Grover Cleveland elected President
1886	Ezra Pound born James, *The Bostonians*	Completion of Canadian Pacific Railway